A **TRUE** BOOK™

NATURAL DISASTER!

All About Volcanoes

Discovering How Earth Erupts

Libby Romero

Children's Press®
An imprint of Scholastic Inc.

Content Consultant
Dr. Kristen Rasmussen
Assistant Professor
Department of Atmospheric Science
Colorado State University

Library of Congress Cataloging-in-Publication Data
Names: Romero, Libby, author.
Title: All about volcanoes / Libby Romero.
Description: First edition. | New York : Children's Press, an imprint of Scholastic Inc., 2021. | Series: A true book: natural disaster! | Includes bibliographical references and index. | Audience: Ages 8–10. | Audience: Grades 4–6. | Summary: "This book shows readers the awesome power of volcanoes"—Provided by publisher.
Identifiers: LCCN 2021003958 (print) | LCCN 2021003959 (ebook) | ISBN 9781338769678 (library binding) | ISBN 9781338769692 (paperback) | ISBN 9781338769708 (ebook)
Subjects: LCSH: Volcanoes—Juvenile literature. | Natural disasters—Juvenile literature.
Classification: LCC QE521.3 .R656 2021 (print) | LCC QE521.3 (ebook) | DDC 551.21—dc23
LC record available at https://lccn.loc.gov/2021003958
LC ebook record available at https://lccn.loc.gov/2021003959

The publisher does not have any control over and does not assume any responsibility for author or third-party websites or their content.

10 9 8 7 6 5 4 3 2 1   22 23 24 25 26

Printed in the U.S.A. 113
First edition, 2022

Series produced by Priyanka Lamichhane
Book design by Kathleen Petelinsek
Illustrations on pages 42–43 by Gary LaCoste

Front cover: Background: Lava flows from a volcano; top: A fiery lava lake at the top of a volcano; top right: Grape vines growing on the side of a composite volcano; bottom: A volcanic eruption seen from space.

Back cover: A cloud of ash drifts out of Mount St. Helens during an eruption.

Find the Truth!

Everything you are about to read is true ***except*** for one of the sentences on this page.

Which one is **TRUE**?

T or F   Volcanoes help keep Earth cooler.

T or F   There are six main types of volcanoes.

Find the answers in this book.

What's in This Book?

The inside of a volcano

4

An illustration of an erupting volcano on an island in Indonesia

The heat from magma can be used to make power in plants like this one.

A Huge Eruption

Mount St. Helens, located in Washington State, is a mountain, but it is also a volcano. It has openings where **lava**, ash, and hot gases can erupt. The volcano had been inactive for 123 years. Then, in March 1980, earthquakes started to shake the ground because **magma** under the volcano began to rise. The magma rose high enough to boil water beneath the surface, creating **steam**. The steam caused **pressure** to build up inside the volcano. **Earthquakes** also kept shaking the area for the next two months.

Mount St. Helens's eruption created the largest landslide in recorded history.

A cloud of ash drifted east after Mount St. Helens erupted. Within 15 days, the ash cloud had circled Earth.

Then, at 8:32 a.m. on May 18, 1980, a bigger earthquake struck, and **Mount St. Helens finally erupted.** Its top and side collapsed, and the pressure that had been building inside was released. Within three minutes, a blast of **hot gas and ash whooshed out** from the side of the volcano. Traveling at more than 300 miles an hour (483 kilometers an hour), it **blew ash and rock** as far as 17 miles (27 km) away. Then, ash and gases rose up high into the air. Mount St. Helens had roared back to life!

A volcano is active if it has erupted in the past 10,000 years.

Volcanoes have three stages: active, dormant, and extinct. Extinct volcanoes will never erupt again.

Understanding Volcanoes

When a volcano erupts, lava and ash can cover entire towns or forests. But lava can also create new land. Volcanoes formed more than 80 percent of Earth's surface, above and below the sea. On land, there are about 1,500 potentially active volcanoes. Scientists think there could be up to one million more on the ocean floor. To understand where and how they form, you have to take a peek inside Earth.

Inside Earth

Earth is made of layers. The top layer is the crust. It contains all of the land on Earth's surface, known as the continental crust. It also contains land on the ocean floor, which is the ocean crust. The layer below the crust is called the mantle. It is divided into upper and lower parts. The mantle sits on top of the liquid outer core, which surrounds the solid inner core at Earth's center.

Earth's Structure

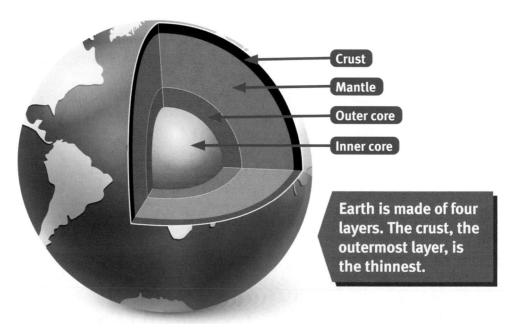

Crust

Mantle

Outer core

Inner core

Earth is made of four layers. The crust, the outermost layer, is the thinnest.

Location of the Ring of Fire

Ring of fire

Seventy-five percent of the active volcanoes on Earth are in the Ring of Fire, which borders tectonic plates in the Pacific Ocean.

When magma reaches Earth's surface, it is called lava.

The crust and top of the mantle form a shell around Earth. Over time, that shell broke into giant pieces called **tectonic plates**. The plates fit together like a puzzle. They move slowly as they float over a soft, partly melted layer of rock in the upper mantle. Most volcanoes form at boundaries, where two plates push against each other or pull apart. Some plates slide past each other, but volcanoes aren't likely to form there.

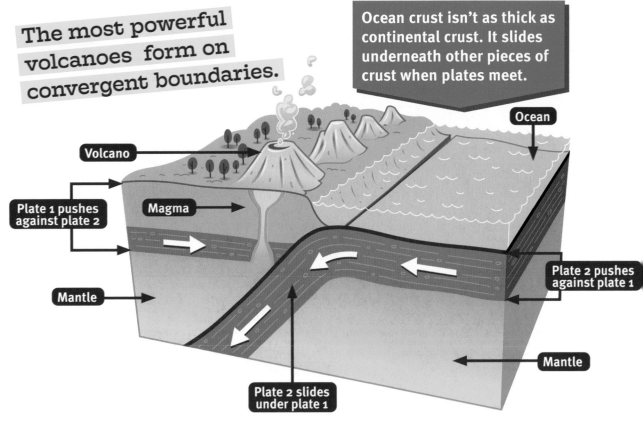

The most powerful volcanoes form on convergent boundaries.

Ocean crust isn't as thick as continental crust. It slides underneath other pieces of crust when plates meet.

Ocean

Volcano

Plate 1 pushes against plate 2

Magma

Plate 2 pushes against plate 1

Mantle

Mantle

Plate 2 slides under plate 1

Convergent Boundaries

A **convergent** boundary is where two plates push against each other. When this happens, one plate slides underneath the other. As the lower plate sinks, rocks in the sinking plate or just above the sinking plate melt to produce some magma. The magma rises through cracks in the crust to form a volcano.

Divergent Boundaries

A **divergent** boundary forms when two tectonic plates move away from each other. As the plates spread apart, they form a valley. The crust in the valley is weak, so it is easy for magma to rise to the surface. When the magma erupts, lava flows out. The lava hardens and builds up to form volcanoes.

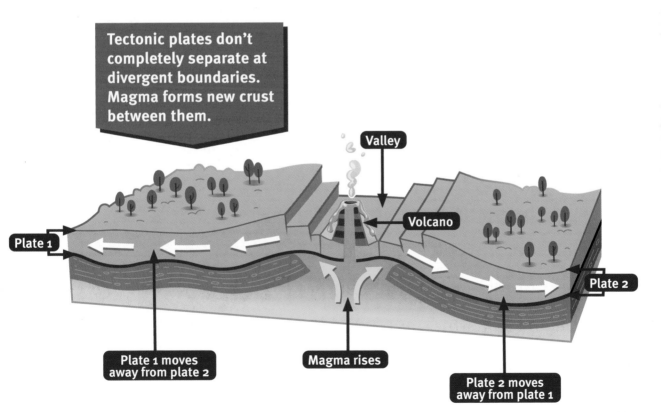

Tectonic plates don't completely separate at divergent boundaries. Magma forms new crust between them.

Valley

Volcano

Plate 1

Plate 2

Plate 1 moves away from plate 2

Magma rises

Plate 2 moves away from plate 1

Hot Spots

Some volcanoes form in the middle of tectonic plates. This happens in **hot spots**. A hot spot is a large column of superhot, partially melted rock that rises from deep within Earth's mantle. The rock breaks through the crust and erupts many times to form a volcano. The hot spot doesn't move, but the plate above it does. In time, the volcano is cut off from its lava source and becomes extinct. A new volcano then forms over the hot spot.

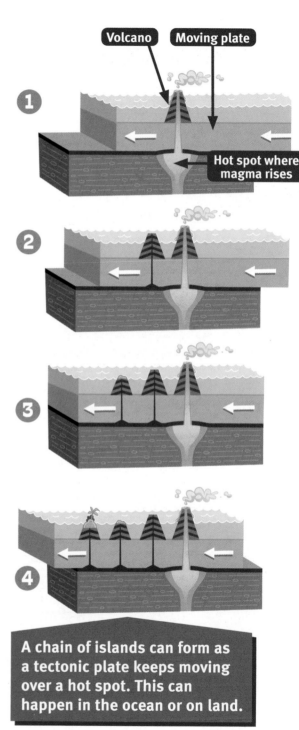

Volcano | Moving plate

Hot spot where magma rises

A chain of islands can form as a tectonic plate keeps moving over a hot spot. This can happen in the ocean or on land.

Hawaiian Islands

The Hawaiian Islands are some of the most well-known hot spot volcanoes. They formed as a tectonic plate inched its way across a hot spot in the Pacific Ocean. Over 70 million years, the moving plate created a long chain of islands and underwater mountains, called seamounts. Together, they stretch out for more than 3,728 miles (6,000 km). The oldest parts of the chain are now near Alaska.

Kauai

Oahu
Molokai
Maui

Hawaii

The main islands of Hawaii

Kauai, the oldest of the main Hawaiian Islands, is no longer above the hot spot. It has no active volcanoes.

The word "volcano" comes from Vulcan, the name for the Roman god of fire.

A large lake of molten lava fills the top of the Erta Ale volcano in the African country of Ethiopia.

Inside a Volcano

At any given time, about 20 volcanoes are erupting somewhere on Earth. Sometimes volcanoes erupt with a big, dangerous bang. Other times they spit out lava so slowly that you could walk faster than it flows. Either way, it all starts with magma. Magma collects in pools called magma chambers that are found deep inside Earth. To learn what happens inside a volcano as it is about to erupt, read on!

How a Volcano Erupts

Normally, magma just collects in a magma chamber. But sometimes, the chamber fills with gases that build up pressure. As the pressure increases, magma is pushed up through the main **vent** toward the surface. It also rises through secondary vents, which are cracks in the middle and sides of a volcano. When the pressure becomes too great, the volcano blows its top, forming an opening called a crater.

Parts of a Volcano

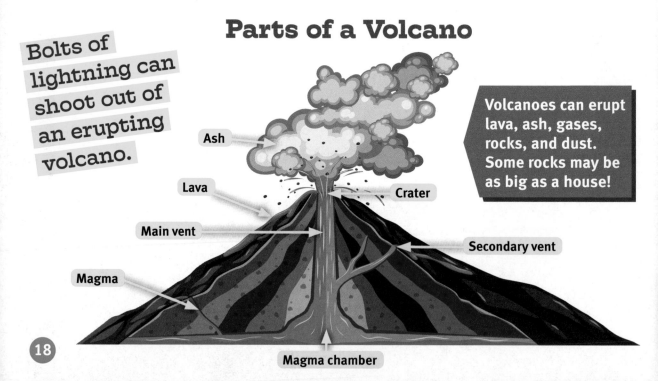

Bolts of lightning can shoot out of an erupting volcano.

Volcanoes can erupt lava, ash, gases, rocks, and dust. Some rocks may be as big as a house!

Ash

Lava

Crater

Main vent

Secondary vent

Magma

Magma chamber

Danger Zone!

Just as interesting as what's inside a volcano is what can come out or can happen when it erupts. Here are a few of the dangers a volcano can create.

Lava flows: These rivers of molten rock bury and burn everything they touch.

Lava bombs: These blobs of lava fly through the air during an eruption.

Gases: Clouds of gas are poisonous and can be the deadliest part of an eruption.

Tsunamis: When volcanoes erupt on the ocean floor, they can trigger these dangerous, fast-moving waves.

Ash falls: These superfine pieces of rock fall in a thick layer that buries everything it covers.

Lahars: When volcanic ash and rocks mix with water from a river, a lake, or melted ice or snow, it creates these volcanic mudflows.

Pyroclastic flows: These fast-moving mixtures of crushed up rock, ash, and hot gases can race down the side of a volcano.

Volcanoes are hot! Volcanologists must wear protective suits when they get up close to them.

Studying Volcanoes

Volcanologists are scientists who study volcanoes. They learn about a volcano's past. Rocks can help them understand how and when a volcano erupted. Volcanologists also study what volcanoes are doing now. They use machines called seismographs to measure earthquakes, which often happen when volcanoes erupt. They have tools to take the temperature of lava. They also study images of volcanoes to monitor them from a safe distance.

Volcanologists use what they learn to try to predict when volcanoes may erupt. This is important because millions of people live near active volcanoes. Warnings save lives. They did in 1995 on the Caribbean island of Montserrat. The island's Soufrière (sue-free-YAIR) Hills volcano became active. Volcanologists warned people when the volcano became dangerous. The people left the island before ash, hot rocks, and mudslides raced down the side of the volcano.

Before 1995, the Soufrière Hills volcano had been dormant for more than 300 years.

After the eruption, Montserrat's capital, Plymouth, ended up buried under layers of ash and mud.

Mount Etna is the most active volcano in Europe.

Mount Etna is a composite volcano in Italy. People have been recording data on its eruptions since 1500 BCE.

3

Types of Volcanoes

Different types of volcanoes are found all over the world. The type is based on how the volcanoes are shaped, which depends on how they formed. Scientists usually separate them into four main kinds: cinder cone, composite, shield, and lava dome. Each type has different characteristics.

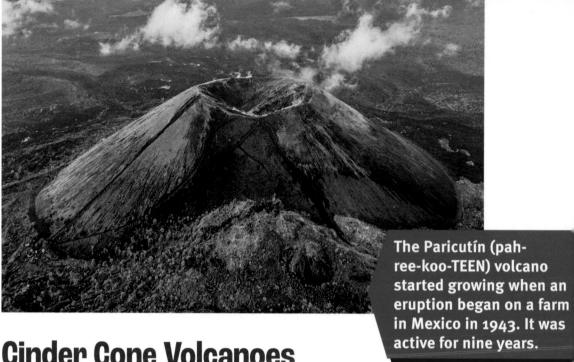

The Paricutín (pah-ree-koo-TEEN) volcano started growing when an eruption began on a farm in Mexico in 1943. It was active for nine years.

Cinder Cone Volcanoes

Cinder cone volcanoes form when lava explodes violently out of a single, central vent, or opening. The lava breaks into pieces as it is thrown into the air. The pieces cool and become solid pieces of rock called cinders. When the cinders fall back down, they settle around the volcano's opening. They build a cone-shaped volcano with a wide, bowl-shaped crater at the top. Some cinder cones grow during one long-lasting eruption and are only active for a few years.

Composite Volcanoes

Some of Earth's biggest mountains are composite volcanoes. These cone-shaped volcanoes have tall, steep sides. Most have a crater at the top. Inside, a network of vents carries magma toward the surface. Composite volcanoes have violent eruptions. Lava may flow through the crater or burst through cracks in the volcano's sides. It grows as lava, cinders, and ash build up on its sides. These volcanoes may erupt thousands of times over millions of years.

Nevados Ojos del Salado (neh-VAH-dohs OH-hohs dehl sah-LAH-doh) is a composite volcano in the Andes Mountains of South America. It is Earth's highest active volcano.

More than 60 percent of all volcanoes are composite volcanoes.

Shield Volcanoes

Shield volcanoes are made almost entirely out of lava. During an eruption, thin, runny lava flows out of vents in all directions. The lava cools into thin layers. Over time, the layers slowly build up to create a broad, gently sloping dome. Shield volcanoes aren't likely to have explosive eruptions. But they do erupt more often than other types of volcanoes.

Mauna Loa (mau-na LOH-ah), a shield volcano in Hawaii, is the most active volcano on Earth.

Guatemala's Santa María volcano erupted in 1902. Lava domes started growing in its crater 20 years later.

Lava Dome Volcanoes

Sometimes lava is so thick that it piles up over a vent instead of flowing out and away. That's how lava dome volcanoes form. They get taller as magma pushes its way up from the inside. As they grow, their outer surface cools and hardens. Then the outer surface shatters, spilling hot rocks down the volcano's sides. These volcanoes continue to grow from within. Lava domes often grow inside craters or on the sides of other volcanoes.

Types of Lava

Lava flows and cools in different ways. This is because not all magma is the same. Magma is melted rock. Different kinds of rocks contain different minerals. Each mineral has unique characteristics. The type of mineral in magma determines how thick lava is, its color, how fast it flows, and the shapes it forms when it cools and hardens.

Pillow lava
This lava erupts slowly from underwater volcanoes. As the lava cools in the water, it forms pillow-shaped rocks.

Pāhoehoe (pah-HOH-ee-HOH-ee) lava
This thin, runny lava flows easily. As it cools it forms a smooth, ropy surface.

ʻAʻā (AH-ah) lava:
This pasty-looking lava is thick enough that the outer layer cools and the inside stays hot as it flows. When the lava hardens, it forms sharp, broken lava blocks called clinkers.

Column lava
This lava cracks into columns as it cools. The columns often have six smooth sides.

Rhyolitic lava
This is the coolest and thickest lava. As magma, it explodes out of a volcano. Rhyolitic lava often forms lava domes.

Volcanoes erupt longer on Mars than they do on Earth.

This illustration shows Olympus Mons. It is a shield volcano on the planet Mars. It is about three times taller than the largest volcano on Earth.

4

Famous Volcanoes

Volcanoes can be considered famous for many reasons. Some are powerful, others are huge. Olympus Mons, a volcano on the planet Mars, is famous for being gigantic. About as wide as the state of Arizona, it's one of the largest known volcanoes in our solar system. There are plenty of famous volcanoes on our own planet, too. Let's take a look at a few of them and learn why they are so well-known.

Mount Vesuvius

In 79 CE, Italy's Mount Vesuvius erupted. A cloud of hot rocks, ash, and gases rose high into the sky. As the cloud cooled, fine ash fell to the ground. Then a pyroclastic flow—a mixture of crushed rock, ash, and hot gases—surged down the side of the volcano. The next day, the nearby city of Pompeii lay buried under at least 16 feet (5 meters) of ash and rocks. The nearby town of Herculaneum was covered with much deeper layers of rocks and mud.

For more than 2,000 years, the ash preserved the city of Pompeii almost exactly as it had been during Roman times.

It's a Supervolcano!

The Yellowstone supervolcano is an extremely large volcano located on top of a hot spot in the northwestern United States. This hot spot has been active for more than 17 million years. In the past 2.1 million years, it has had at least three major eruptions. Each eruption was powerful enough to make the volcano collapse and form a **caldera**, or giant bowl-shaped dip, in the ground.

The colorful Grand Prismatic Spring is the largest hot spring in Yellowstone National Park. It is located on the western part of the third caldera (see location below).

Yellowstone National Park

FIRST CALDERA
(formed 2.1 million years ago)

SECOND CALDERA
(formed 1.3 million years ago)

Grand Prismatic Spring

THIRD CALDERA
(formed 640,000 years ago)

Mount Tambora

Mount Tambora, located on a small Indonesian island, erupted in 1815. The powerful eruption blew ash and gases into the atmosphere, blocking sunlight. The deadly haze lowered temperatures and changed Earth's climate for three years. Colder temperatures and less sunshine killed crops around the world. People died of hunger and disease. Many volcanologists consider this to be the most destructive volcanic event in recorded history.

Timeline of Volcanic Eruptions

640,000 YEARS AGO
Yellowstone has its most recent major eruption.

79 CE
Mount Vesuvius erupts in Italy, burying the city of Pompeii.

1815
Mount Tambora explodes in Indonesia, leading to "the year without summer."

1883
Krakatau erupts in Indonesia, causing one of the deadliest eruptions in modern history.

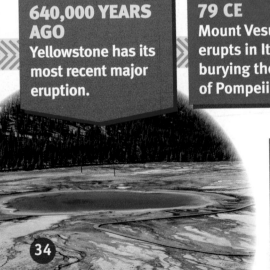

Krakatau

In August 1883, a volcano on the tiny Indonesian island of Krakatau (krak-uh-TAO) erupted. It blasted rocks and ash miles into the air. The eruption is estimated to have killed more than 36,000 people. It was one of the deadliest volcanic eruptions in modern history. Most people drowned after the volcano collapsed into a caldera and several **tsunamis** raced across the sea.

1902
Santa María volcano erupts in Guatemala, slowly forming lava domes. They are still active today.

1943
Paricutín, one of the youngest volcanoes on Earth, emerges in a cornfield in Mexico.

1980
Mount St. Helens erupts, destroying homes and the surrounding land, and even stopping airplane traffic due to all the ash in the air.

1995
Soufrière Hills volcano becomes active on the island of Montserrat in the Caribbean.

Gases and water vapor from early volcanoes helped form Earth's atmosphere.

In 2009, astronauts in space saw this eruption of the Sarychev volcano. It is located on the Kuril Islands, northeast of Japan.

The Impact of Volcanoes

Volcanoes can do a lot of damage, but they also help Earth. Volcanoes erupt lava, which forms new land. They release water vapor, a gas, which turns into water when it cools. Volcanoes also release other gases and particles into the atmosphere that lower global temperatures by blocking some of the sun's heat from reaching Earth's surface. This gives Earth a short break from rising temperatures as **global warming** gets worse.

Building Blocks

Volcanoes help form many of the products people use every day. Deep underground, their heat helps create mineral resources such as copper and gold. On the surface, volcanic rocks and ash break down. People use these materials to make everything from concrete and roofing products to hand soaps and household cleaners. As cooled lava and ash break down, they also produce rich soils where people can grow food.

Grape vines grow in the fertile soil on the side of this composite volcano in Spain.

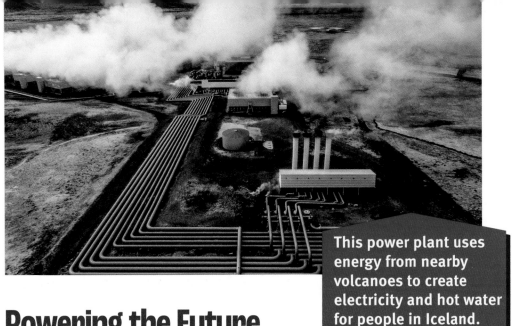

This power plant uses energy from nearby volcanoes to create electricity and hot water for people in Iceland.

Powering the Future

Volcanoes give people a natural way to make electricity without hurting the environment. Magma heats water in underground springs near volcanoes. The boiling hot water makes steam. People drill holes to get hot water and steam from the ground. This is called **geothermal energy**. It is a renewable form of heat that can continuously power the planet. Using sources of clean energy like this can help protect our planet from pollution. Volcanoes are really powerful. And they can help us power the future!

Mapping Volcanoes

Most volcanoes form where tectonic plates push together or move apart. Others form in hot spots. But what exactly does that mean when you're looking at a map? This map shows where many of Earth's major volcanoes are located. Study it, and then answer the questions that follow.

Analyze It!

1. Where do most of the volcanoes on this map occur?

2. Which tectonic plate is surrounded by the Ring of Fire?

3. On which coast are all the volcanoes in South America located?

4. Is a volcano more likely to appear on the East Coast or West Coast of the United States? Why?

Earth's Major Volcanoes and Tectonic Plates

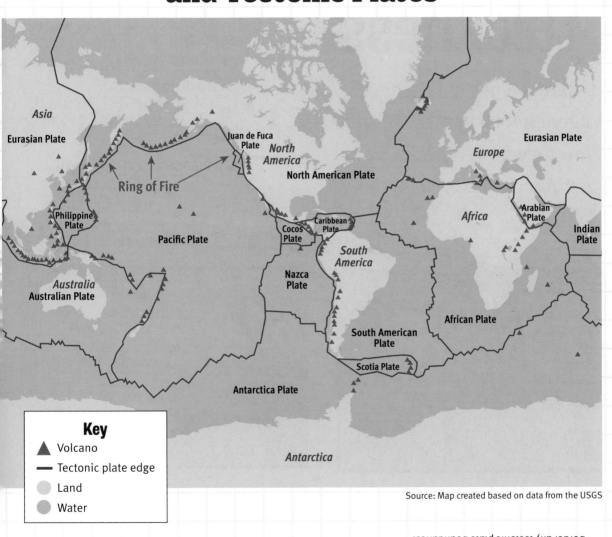

Asia

Eurasian Plate

Juan de Fuca Plate

North America

North American Plate

Europe

Eurasian Plate

Ring of Fire

Philippine Plate

Pacific Plate

Cocos Plate

Caribbean Plate

South America

Africa

Arabian Plate

Indian Plate

Australia

Australian Plate

Nazca Plate

South American Plate

African Plate

Scotia Plate

Antarctica Plate

Antarctica

Key
▲ Volcano
— Tectonic plate edge
Land
Water

Source: Map created based on data from the USGS

Test Lava Thickness

Different types of lava have different thicknesses. This affects how they flow. Here's a simple test you can do to learn more.

Materials

Four tall, thin, clear glasses

Four clear liquids of different thicknesses, such as water, vegetable oil, dishwashing soap, and honey

Piece of paper

Pen

Timer

Four pebbles of the same size

Directions

liquid	flow	prediction	time
water	fast	1 sec.	
oil	fast	1 sec.	
soap	slow	4 sec.	
honey	slow	12	

1 Fill each glass to the top with a different liquid. Observe the liquids as you pour them to see how easily they flow. Write your observations down.

2 Based on your observations, predict what will happen when you drop a pebble in each glass. Record your predictions.

3 Start the timer as you drop a pebble in the first glass. Stop the timer when the pebble reaches the bottom. Record the results.

4 Repeat step 3 with the remaining liquids.

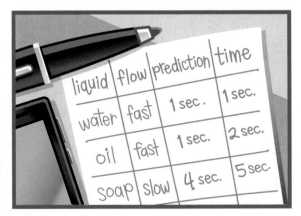

liquid	flow	prediction	time
water	fast	1 sec.	1 sec.
oil	fast	1 sec.	2 sec.
soap	slow	4 sec.	5 sec.

5 Compare the results. Did they match your predictions? What do your results tell you about different types of lava and how they flow?

Explain It!

Using what you learned in the book, can you explain what happened and why? If you need help, turn back to pages 28 and 29.

True Statistics

Temperature of lava: Up to 2,120 degrees Fahrenheit (1,160 degrees Celsius)

Speed of fastest lava flow ever recorded: 37 mph (60 kph)

Number of active volcanoes in the Ring of Fire: About 450

Number of potentially active volcanoes in the United States: 169

Height Mount St. Helens lost when it erupted in 1980: 1,300 feet (396 m)

How far tectonic plates move each year: 1 to 6 inches (2.5 to 15 cm)

Height of Mauna Loa: 13,677 feet (4,169 m) above sea level and 39,000 feet (11,900 m) from the ocean floor

Did you find the truth?

(T) Volcanoes help keep Earth cooler.

(F) There are six main types of volcanoes.

Resources

Other books in this series:

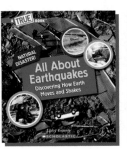   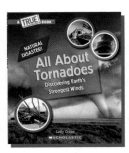 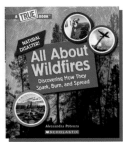

You can also look at:

Hamalainen, Karina. *Hawai'i Volcanoes*. New York: Children's Press, 2019.

Landau, Elaine. *Volcanoes*. New York: Children's Press, 2009.

Morey, Allan. *Supervolcano Eruption*. New York: Bellwether Media, 2019.

Nargi, Lela. *Absolute Expert: Volcanoes*. Washington, D.C.: National Geographic Kids Books, 2018.

Van Rose, Susanna. *Volcano and Earthquake*. New York: DK Children's, 2014.

Woolf, Alex. *The Science of Natural Disasters: The Devastating Truth About Volcanoes, Earthquakes, and Tsunamis*. New York: Children's Press, 2018.

Glossary

caldera (KAL-dare-uh) a giant bowl-shaped dip in the ground formed when a volcano erupts and collapses

convergent (kahn-VUR-jent) tending to move toward each other

divergent (di-VUR-jent) tending to move away from each other

geothermal energy (gee-oh-THER-mal EN-er-gee) heat produced deep inside Earth

global warming (GLOH-buhl WOR-ming) a gradual rise in the temperature of Earth's atmosphere, caused by human activities that release greenhouse gases

hot spots (haht spahtz) places deep within Earth where hot magma rises to just beneath the surface, creating bulges and volcanic activity

lava (LAH-vuh) hot, liquid rock that pours out of a volcano when it erupts; solid rock forms when lava cools

magma (MAG-muh) melted rock found beneath Earth's surface that becomes lava when it flows out of volcanoes

tectonic plates (tek-TAH-nik playts) huge sections of Earth's crust and topmost mantle layer that move very slowly

tsunamis (tsu-NAH-meez) fast-moving and dangerous waves caused by underwater earthquakes or volcanoes

vent (vent) the opening in a volcano through which smoke and lava escape

Index

Page numbers in **bold** indicate illustrations.

About the Author

Libby Romero was a journalist and teacher before becoming an author. She studied agricultural journalism at the University of Missouri-Columbia (BS and BJ) and received her Master of Education from Marymount University in Arlington, Virginia. As a child, she read nearly every nonfiction book in her school's library. Now she's added dozens of new books to the shelves. She lives in Virginia with her husband and two sons.

A *TRUE* BOOK

✷ NATURAL DISASTER! ✷
All About
Volcanoes

Is it true that at any given time about 20 volcanoes are erupting somewhere on Earth?

Yes! Sometimes volcanoes erupt with a big, dangerous bang. Other times they spit out lava so slowly that you could walk faster than it flows.

INSIDE, YOU'LL FIND:

✷ How volcanoes form, when they erupt, and an account of the most devastating ones in recent history;

✷ A hands-on activity, a timeline, photos, diagrams—and how scientists are studying volcanoes and their impact on our planet;

✷ Surprising TRUE facts that will shock and amaze you!

All NEW! All TRUE!

Children's Press® an imprint of

📖 **SCHOLASTIC**

scholastic.com/library publishing

ISBN 978-1-338-76969-2

$7.99 US
$9.99 CAN

9 781338 769692